Jean Frémon

David Hockney in his Studio

Translated by Jacob Bromberg

Hermits United
London · Paris

Published in Great Britain by Hermits United Ltd. 2025

Translated from Jean Frémon, *David Hockney à l'atelier*
(L'Échoppe, 2017)

English translation © Hermits United 2025

All rights reserved
Printed in Europe

A catalogue record for this book is available from the British Library
ISBN 978-1-916658-11-0

www.hermits-united.com

David Hockney in his Studio

I

Los Angeles, 1998–2001.

David Hockney's house is something of an artwork in its own right. It sits on Montcalm Avenue, a small residential street off Mulholland Drive, the long road that winds along the top of the canyon overlooking the city. At night, you can see a vast and shimmering field, a grid of boulevards – Sunset, Hollywood, Santa Monica – and avenues cutting across one another. Even though he is not the first to have lived there, he has made the house a work of art, taking possession of it by suffusing the space with his playful intelligence. From the outside, there is nothing to see but a small unremarkable doorway; the house itself is not visible from the street. Once you step past this gateway, there are a few steps painted blue immediately to the right that lead down to the house's landing door, while on the left, a paved path lined with flowerbeds leads slightly uphill towards the studio. The house, like many others here, is actually built into the canyon – it is set back against the escarpment, below road level, and opens onto a several-hundred-metre slope on the other side, offering an unobstructed view of the canyon's luxuriant foliage: palm trees, banana trees, agaves, and more.

The first thing that strikes you upon walking into the house is a patio door on the right that gives onto the nearby hillside, light streaming in from above. It is a lush green space, but because the incline is so steep, it remains inaccessible and acts simply as a backdrop. And so, Hockney transformed it into an aquarium. An aquarium of his own making, of course – with no water. He drew colourful fish on cut wooden boards and hung them at various heights outside, behind the glass, creating not a true aquarium but a fictional one that can only be seen from within the house. The shrubs and grasses growing there thus become underwater plants, caught up in the fiction despite themselves And so we have already entered into David Hockney's world – the realm of representation.

On the right sits a grand piano with scores always open atop it. I don't know who plays it; I've never asked. Behind the piano is a bookcase containing, among other things, the complete Zervos set of Picasso's catalogue raisonné. All of Picasso in black and white: the best way to analyse the structure of the works. There's no tiring of it, and Hockney is no exception in this; he returns to the books again and again, drawing his visitors to them as well.

A few sofas are arranged in front of the fireplace to the left as you enter, with Stanley and Boogie, the two dachshunds, lounging on them. Hockney has painted them extensively in all their slouching poses – some 50 small canvases whose dimensions allow the artist to paint one or both dogs at life-size, sprawled out on that same yellow cushion. The mantlepiece is decorated in *trompe-l'œil* by the master of the house: a profile drawing of Louis XVI in a wig, a garland of peppers in grisaille, painted candlesticks – even the dogs' portrait imitates a family photo leaned back against the mantelpiece. Not only are we in a world of fictions, but we are surrounded by plays on perspective. Rather than tricking the eye, it amuses.

The room is immense, combining a sitting area, a

dining room with a circular table that could easily seat ten people, and an open-plan kitchen giving onto a bar behind which a Mexican chef is working busily. This living room, which has no ceiling, sitting open to the rafters, has been the subject of countless paintings in which Hockney plays with perspective and the memory of Cubism to produce the improbable yet lively spaces he is so adept at creating, such as *Large Interior, Los Angeles*, 1998. A long sliding glass door opens onto a wooden balcony painted in blue and red – two intense colours that bring out the green of the surrounding foliage. A multitude of potted plants – cacti, hibiscus, orchids, and more – sit on the balcony guardrail. This balcony and these potted plants have likewise been the subject of many colourful paintings by the artist. The balcony leads to an *opus incertum* paved pathway connecting the house to the printmaking studio: the realm of Maurice Payne, whose face resembles that of a daydreaming eagle, his hair standing straight upright, his speech reserved. Inside the small, independent house of the printmaking studio, we admired proofs of the latest prints – mostly aquatints of bouquets of flowers in black and white. Was there some perverse desire at work here, seeking to frustrate the flower-lover who would never imagine buying a blossom without its colours? Perhaps a taste for the paradoxical? More likely, the excitement of a challenge: to successfully render the feeling of colour, *sans* colour.

Looking down and to the left from the balcony, one can see the bean-shaped pool whose bottom Hockney painted with large blue arcs that mimic the movements of water.

The studio is distinct from the house – it is on street level, on the left as you enter the space, and at the end of a paved pathway lined with flowers that was the subject of a series of large charcoal drawings: close-ups of cacti, ferns, and daturas in flower, hanging in bunches. Hockney delights in a challenge, as I've said. What he has achieved as a print he tries anew in charcoal. As much as he loves and makes unsparing use of colour, he also loves to realise such feats as creating the impression – indeed, the feeling – of colour while using only the black of the charcoal and the grain of the white paper. The Chinese knew how to do it – Hockney shall, too. That same corner of the garden, near the pool, was drawn twice with the same framing on sheets of paper with the same dimensions; the first drawing was made early in the morning, the second in late afternoon the same day. In both cases, using only charcoal, Hockney manages to render totally different atmospheres of light – the masses of plants are the same, and yet the light captured by the charcoal is so dissimilar that you have to look twice to be sure the view is truly identical.

Immersed in greenery, the studio is a vast, high-ceilinged rectangular room with a wooden mezzanine at the far end. A series of tables placed end to end along the length of the wall bears computers, a printer, a slide viewer, a scanner, a photocopier, lightboxes – everything the state of the art in technology can offer. David Hockney is never behind the times: he has the means to procure the latest innovations and constantly takes advantage of all that technological progress can afford, putting it in the service of his insatiable curiosity. A sign, written in the painter's hand – drawn, even – insists that visitors take no photos or videos, encouraging them instead to look with their own eyes.

Reproductions of the most remarkable paintings in the history of art are pinned up along the length of the back wall, arranged by half-century. We witness the figure slowly emerge from the icon, and then, precisely between 1420 and 1430, take on a more singular personality: observation of the real model gradually takes precedence over the ideal. The gesture gains the ability to express an emotion, gaze and smile are suddenly coordinated, and the painted figure soon appears to truly be looking out at the viewer. This journey, through Christs, Madonnas, saints, lords, popes, doges, and merchants, has never been seen like this before, unfurled like a Chinese scroll. It is a procession, a parade – everything is orderly and chronological: the Arnolfini couple holding hands precedes the enigmatic Mona Lisa, who narrowly precedes the proud Balthazar Castiglione, who precedes the restrained Mademoiselle Rivière, soon followed by the unsophisticated Joseph Roulin, and then by Gertrude with her almond-shaped eyes. But it can all be seen at once, as though all this history were present and contemporary. Which, of course, it is for us, as History and as a succession of histories; but this single wall makes the fact obvious for the first time, because we no longer need turn pages or pull a hundred heavy tomes from library shelves. We can see the kinships and caesuras unfold over time with naked eye, like in a diagram that traces the evolution of animal species. Just as one can see the moment when primate stands upright to walk on two legs and begins to take human form, on this wall we see the moment when the eye truly begins to look, when the face becomes singular, when the real overthrows the ideal. This fresco of the greatest masterpieces in the history of painting, or at least of figures, is almost exclusively composed of portraits. Hockney is very much at home with portraiture. And the figure's gaze in the portrait says a great deal about the painter's own gaze. The whole of art history is contemporary to us, and Hockney ambles freely through it, drawing new ways of seeing and new modes of expression from what stands out to him. He mixes styles unabashedly, appropriates manners as he pleases, and always with a sense of humour.

Leaving the studio to return to the house, I attempted to find the subjects of the drawings I had just seen among the flowerbeds. David stopped me at the threshold of the studio and said, 'Look left, look right, then look up in the air', and then, 'Don't you like seeing things bigger?' It's an obsession with Hockney – bigger, always bigger: *A Bigger Splash*, *A Bigger Canyon*. To the famous Minimalist credo *less is more*, Hockney retorts *bigger is better*. The term megalomania denotes a kind of personality disorder with which we are all familiar. Hockney is worlds away from that. Perhaps instead we should speak of megalophilia. He loves to see things big, and bigger yet – and he gives himself licence to do so. In *The Gate*, that view from the door of the studio that gives onto the house (of which we can scarce see anything but the purple roof behind trunks and branches painted in a kind of voluminous pointillism), he did paint the view as it is, but he enlarged it, adding to the painting what one sees upon lifting one's gaze skyward and turning it both left and right. I exhibited that painting in Paris, in 2001, and I will never forget the enthusiasm of the person who bought it – a small, energetic and intelligent woman who has since passed. She knocked on the door to my office after having seen the show in the gallery. She had never bought such a large and expensive work before. She said, 'It's mad, but I can't help it. I simply have to buy it. I can't do otherwise. You and I are going to call up my banker – you'll see, he'll say I've gone mad, but he'll have to do what I tell him. I'll pass the phone to you and you'll just have to give him your account number and the price. He'll be flabbergasted, you'll see.' This small woman was overjoyed at the idea of playing a good trick on everybody – her family, her banker – by indulging what others would call a whim but which for her was simply a moral obligation to honour her sudden enchantment. Seeing big – thinking big – is contagious.

When I was a child, an invention came along that completely changed cinema; it came from America and was called a CinemaScope. I imagine that made an impression on David Hockney, too: he translates everything into CinemaScope.

But there are more surprises to come. In the garden adjoining the studio, Hockney had a plywood hut built in which he created total darkness by covering the openings with black tarpaulins. Just one single square hole was made in one of the walls. Outside, in front of this small window, he has arranged elements of a still life as they were popularly painted in the seventeenth century: an apple, a cabbage hanging by a thread, an open melon, and a cucumber. His model is a painting from 1602 by Juan Sánchez Cotán, the painter of the *bodégons*, held by the San Diego Museum of Art. The fruits have been placed on a small wooden stand at window level. Inside the dark hut, on the wall facing the window, he has placed a mirror on a slightly skewed axis. This mirror projects a perfect inverse reflection of what appears outside the window onto the wall across from it: the still life in full sunlight. All the painter has to do is pin a piece of paper to the wall and trace the contours of the projection with his pencil.

This was the first time I had ever seen an image reflected this way in a *camera obscura*. I defy anyone not to immediately think of Vermeer or Chardin in response to such a sight. The reflected image has a luminous intensity that far outstrips reality. This is to be expected, of course – it is made entirely of light, *sine materia*. The outlines of the objects are blurred by a kind of vibrating halo that magnifies them. In reality, it is the objects, these fruits, that receive and reflect sunlight; in the reflected image, to the contrary, we have the impression that light is emanating from the object itself. And since the contours of the reflected image are slightly blurry and trembling, we feel as though the object itself were breathing, shining – as though the soul of nature had become visible. The bread on the lace-maker's table, Zurbarán's glass of water, and Chardin's fruit all have this luminous depth, like the light of a sapphire or an emerald, an impalpable, vibrant thickness. There is no doubt these painters used *camerae obscurae* and were intrigued, indeed seduced, by the images they produce – seduced to the point of wanting to paint not the still life itself but the so much more vivid image created in the dark room. And this image offers yet another advantage: it has only two dimensions – it is flat; its depth is already fictitious. In other words, it is halfway between reality and the canvas the artist will go on to paint. The trick, as Hockney points out, is to capture the light in the painted surface; that is to say, to bring spirit into the material.

After having tested the process with a melon and a cabbage, Hockney had one of his friends pose in the sunlight, in front of the window of the *camera obscura*: a three-quarter profile, like the portrait of Cardinal Albergati painted by Van Eyck in 1431, with the same red chasuble, the same corpulent face. Inside the dark room, the painter makes a few marks, following the inversed reflection. What is the point of this method? To more quickly capture an expression, he says. Expressions are fleeting – if you want to get both the eyes and the mouth, you have to be quick. A few marks for reference points suffice to ensure the proportions are perfect, improving on the estimation of dimensions with one's thumb on a pencil stretched out in front of you while closing one eye, as students are taught to do. However, it is no art historian undertaking this exercise to understand how the great artists of the past did things – it is a painter, a practitioner, who wants to know, to understand, to replicate and push further. Historians work in libraries, practitioners recreate experiments. The test of facts is more compelling than erudition. And don't think it's not necessary to know how to draw because one can simply follow the outlines of the projected reflection; if you are a bad draughtsman, your drawing will be bad, reflection or no, he says with certainty.

*

Lunch break. The table is equipped with the kind of rotating centre you find in Chinese restaurants – all the dishes are in the middle and everyone takes a turn serving themselves. Today's menu: sushi, sashimi, and California rolls in abundance. Hockney drinks a light beer, having kept alcohol at a certain distance since a bout with pancreatitis.

A bottle of Evian sits on the table. Hockney, who hunts the mysteries of transparency wherever he might find them, turns the bottle towards me and says, 'Look, it says *naïve*!'

*

Suddenly, near the end of the afternoon, David gets up and says, 'Come, let's go for a drive.' We follow him. He tells us to get into his car – a red Mercedes convertible. Hockney has never been afraid of colour. It is a beautiful day out. He puts on a white baseball cap, ties a scarf around his neck, calls out to Stanley, who climbs into the car, and off we go on Mulholland Drive. We head towards the San Gabriel Mountains along the canyons. David drives slowly, concentrated on the task at hand. He remains silent, which is rather rare for him; because of his profound hearing impairment, he usually tends to dominate conversation rather than being obliged to ask others to repeat themselves.

David presses a button that turns on a musical programme. The sound is powerful. The car is equipped with a luxury sound system, and the music we hear brings to mind Leonard Bernstein, and then Gershwin – a medley, a collage of standards that creates a lively, energetic mood. David turns the sound up louder, seeming to relish the effect. This light-hearted beginning to our musical jaunt seems a warm-up, an appetiser of sorts. As the landscape becomes truly spectacular, we come to the serious stuff. Strauss, I believe – *Also Sprach Zarathustra*. Great tearing notes from the string section supported by cymbals and drum rolls coincide precisely with the rise and fall of a mountain peak on our left and then our right, with a vertiginous opening between two ridges. The postcard landscape is full of contrasts: red and yellow earth, submerged in shadow and violently illuminated. Now it's Wagner, there's no doubt about it – the shimmering, oscillating strings in a polyphony without melody fuse with the wavering light of a hot, dry late afternoon. Thanks to the sunroof, we are truly there in the space: the wind whips our cheeks and ruffles our hair as we look before us, left, and right, with the feeling that the sky above us is infinite. Stanley loves this, and lifts his chin up to take in the air before curling up on the driver's lap. We can feel the explosion brewing. Little by little, the orchestra swells, expands, extends as the landscape before our eyes grows larger, and larger still. Suddenly, the brass section erupts – at the precise moment the setting sun appears between two peaks overlooking the sea, at the end of Sunset Boulevard, above the cliffs of Pacific Palisades. The light has an extreme precision to it, creating intense contrasts between the dark green of the forests, the yellow of the fields, and the sea in the distance.

David is beaming. 'I asked God to take care of the lighting. He's good, isn't he?'

The act is perfectly polished. The musical montage matches the grandiose landscape to the quarter-second as it unfurls before our eyes. David knows when to slow down and when to speed up in order to be at the right place at the right time. All he has to do is make sure there won't be too much traffic that day. But while Sunset Boulevard is usually congested on the westbound side every evening from 5 p.m. onwards – at night, you can see that immense, radiant serpent stretching all the way out to Venice from far off – the Pacific Coast Highway usually flows freely.

We return through the lower part of the city, as though to avoid dampening the impression of the trip out by driving back in the other direction without the music. Hockney is satisfied with his demonstration. Music, time, space, light. He is in his element: the world, at the crossroads of all the senses – despite the fact that the exercise causes him suffering (because his deafness is a serious impairment and he can no longer hear bass frequencies). He knows perfectly well where the double bass and cello come in when listening to a composition, but he simply cannot hear them anymore. As enjoyable as it is, the little number that weaves Wagner into the Californian landscape is a simulation; he likes to share it with friends, but he knows that music is over for him, and it saddens him. He no longer goes to concerts or to the opera despite having worked so often in that environment. He has grieved his loss of music.

This living script is the last impulse of a music lover who has been abandoned by music. It is present in his memory, but has stopped thrilling his eardrums. Music is no longer physical for him, now only mental, and Hockney cannot be satisfied by sound that has become lacklustre to his ears. But he still has his eyes, his sense of space, of colours, and of light, which he so finely developed while working on his stages and sets for the opera. Now, though, he is not mastering a representation of space but nature itself, or at least a grandiose fragment of it – the snaking road, the peaks, the valleys, the sea, and the daylight that colours them all differently with the passing hours. It is the pleasure of a demiurge.

II

London and Bridlington, July 2003.

As agreed, I call around 10 a.m. to make an appointment for the afternoon. 4 p.m., David tells me. 'Are you staying overnight?' 'No', I reply, 'I have to be at Waterloo Station at 7 p.m.' 'Let's say 3:30, then', he says. I expect that he'll still be in bed if I get there at 3:30. I arrive right on time and hang around Pembroke Gardens, at the entrance to Pembroke studios, for a good 15 minutes before walking down an alleyway lined with blooming lavender to ring the doorbell. David Graves opens the door. David is having a nap. At 4 p.m. sharp, he comes downstairs, wearing red suspenders and a shirt open to the navel. I've brought a bottle of Dom Pérignon and David Freedberg's latest book, *The Eye of the Lynx*, which I had purchased that morning at a bookshop on Charing Cross Road. It's a nice day out, so we go to sit in the garden. David doesn't look at the champagne, which remains on the table in the garden until the end of our meeting, but he dives into the book immediately. He begins reading aloud: 'Had I all the time in the world (and readers all patience), I would have liked to have written more specifically than I have here about the relations between truth and dissimulation, and above all about not telling the truth in order to tell the truth. But that would have meant writing another book entirely – and this one is long enough…'

It was Hockney who had given me Freedberg's *The Power of Images* some years earlier, and now he scours through the table of contents:

The Telescope: Imperfection in the Heavens

The Microscope and the Vernacular

The Fate of Pictures: Appearance, Truth, and Ambiguity

I ask Hockney if he knows Freedberg personally. His reply: 'I met him once, three or four years ago. I had been told he was writing something about lenses.' This was during a period when Hockney was passionate about optical instruments and their use by painters – everything he wrote about in *Secret Knowledge*.

*

Hockney has returned from a trip to Norway, where he made *plein air* watercolours. 'We went as far as the Arctic Circle. Last century, they knew that you spend the winter in the South, the Promenade des Anglais... and in the summer, you go up North. The days are longer. There are these long shadows you can't find anywhere else. The sun is low for five or six hours – you can really look at nature, study shadows. That moment only lasts for five minutes in Los Angeles: the sun sets and disappears, that's that.'

He shows me a small watercolour of the sun hanging low over the horizon of the sea. The sun is made of concentric circles. 'If you look – and you actually can look at the sun at this time of day because it's not so bright – if you really look, you can see circles. Photography will never show you that – it will show you radiance, but not the circles. When children draw a sun, they start by making a circle.' And here, he takes a piece of paper and traces a childlike sun on it. 'And the reflection!' 'Munch saw it', I say. 'Ah, Munch. What a painter. He's up there with Van Gogh – a master.'

David leads me into the studio. Pages from his notebooks brought back from Norway are pinned to the wall: the sun on the fjord, a house on the fjord, fishers, silhouettes in brush and ink... The world of Knut Hamsun. Hockney is no tourist, but he hungers to paint new subjects, new light, new reflections. He travels to find them, to observe and to paint them.

*

'I was looking at Rembrandt, at his drawings. The Chinese would have called him "Master" – his brush heavy with ink, his hand, wrist, arm, shoulder. And what speed! Nobody can hold a candle to him.'

Just then, he goes off to find three massive books published by Phaidon and leafs through them for me, marvelling at each of the drawings reproduced within. 'Just a few quick strokes, and yet an expression on every face. An old woman in front of a fire, warming her hands. They look a bit like lobster claws, and yet they're just right. And this one here, looking at her jealously, she has the best place, right in front of the fire. And this other one who isn't looking, who refuses to look – she's furious. All of this on a paltry piece of paper not more than 15 centimetres long.'

'Oh, you have to see what I did in Los Angeles.' He brings over a large folder filled with photos of watercolours painted that spring. Views from the garden, the cacti in front of the red brick wall, the wooden terrace painted red and blue (in fiction and reality).

The most striking piece is a vertical double-sheet watercolour of rain on the terrace. The rain is rendered by vertical white lines made from the white of the paper. 'Only in Los Angeles is the rain vertical. If you ask a child in London or Japan to draw rain, they'll always draw it in oblique lines. In Los Angeles, there's no wind, so when the rain falls, it comes straight down.'

The drawing of vertical lines to make the rain and the bounce of the large raindrops where they hit the ground (on three levels: the terrace itself, the painted red stool, and the edge of the wooden railing) was first made with gum arabic, appearing colourless and serving to repel the watercolour when applied. The rest of the watercolour follows, making the rain and the bouncing drops appear as a negative with the white of the paper.

The second watercolour depicts the same view after the rain. There are no bouncing raindrops nor vertical lines of rain – everything is calm and peaceful; but the terrace, railing, and stool are still wet and shining with reflections of light. Hockney's watercolour captures this masterfully.

He has even captured how the fact that these surfaces are wet modifies the geometry of their outlines: they are less sharp, more blurred, softer due to the reflection of light in several directions caused by the water's curvature on the edges of objects like the bench or the stool.

He is impatient to return to Los Angeles to paint. 'I'm going to use what I've learned from watercolour in painting. But you can't do the same thing with two different techniques. This glass of water in front of me – if I were to draw it in pencil or paint it in Indian ink, or with watercolours, or oil paints, it wouldn't be the same glass of water at all. And yet, at best, none of them would be untrue.'

Of Rembrandt, he says: 'He has everything a Master needs: the hand, the eye, and the heart.'

*

The sense of incompleteness, knowing how to lift one's hand, to not belabour the work. He recites:
A careless shoe-string, in whose tie
I see a wild civility;
Do more bewitch me than when art
Is too precise in every part.
                       Robert Herrick, *Delight in Disorder*

*

'Happy paintings are not made by happy people', says DH as he shows me an unsparing self-portrait he has just made.

*

'The multiplying villainies of nature.' (Macbeth)

Strange images of death (I note without comment, words heard from his mouth).

*

Bridlington, 2006.

The studio in the fields. Hockney decided to paint *en plein air* views of the Yorkshire countryside, his native landscape. Painting *en plein air* implies painting rather quickly, because the light shifts, so it requires a bit of organisation. You can't bring a canvas larger than the boot of a station wagon into the countryside. In any case, over a certain size, it catches too much wind and the first real gust would take it flying. Hockney is pained by this fact; he like to see big – as big as possible. There must be some way to make it work... And here it is: an even number of small canvases arranged next to one another and painted one after the other so as to create a larger painting all together. The logistics follow: the station wagon's boot has shelves to slide the little paintings in horizontally and allow them to dry as they are painted. Hockney works on several at once because he wants to capture the main lines of the composition, the light, and the spirit of the place; there will always be time in the studio to make any necessary retouches, to perfect the junctures between adjoining canvases. Why go to all this trouble, you may ask? Painting in the studio means transposing a mental image onto canvas – the image comes from memory and sensibility. It is certainly very interesting as an exercise, but very different from one that consists in creating a two-dimensional image from the immense, profuse, confused reality that stands before us in three dimensions. This incomparably more difficult exercise is what holds Hockney's attention for the moment. Hence his studio in the fields.

And, as ever, he needs to see things bigger: assembling 50 panels, Hockney creates the largest painting ever made outdoors. *Bigger Trees Near Warter*, which measures four and a half metres tall and twelve metres long, will go on to occupy the largest wall in the Royal Academy all on its own. He humorously gives it a French subtitle: *Peinture sur le motif pour le nouvel-âge post-photographique*.

*

Late August, 2007.

The 50 panels that compose *Bigger Trees Near Warter* occupy the end wall of the largest gallery at the Royal Academy: ten panels wide, five high. It is March and spring is announced by a few groups of daffodils in the foreground, but the trees have yet to come back into leaf. The trunks and branches stand out clearly. The composition is rather symmetrical: the largest of the trees stands dead centre, its main branches rising and then levelling out almost horizontally on either side of the trunk, giving it the look of a cross. To the left and right of the central tree are two small coppices. It looks like a crucifixion without a victim, and with a cross for a thief to either side, but with no thieves. I make this comment to David and he smiles. 'Yes, it does have some resemblance to Grünewald, doesn't it?' he replies. The twist and orientation of the branches in Hockney's painting is similar to those of Christ's arms in the Isenheim Altarpiece.

On the large walls to either side of it, Hockney has hung two life-size photographic reproductions of the painting. This way, when you face the painting to look at it, you are flanked by the same image both left and right, as though you are in a clearing in the middle of the forest. The painting's triptych composition, already reinforced by the concave movement of the treetops, is heightened by the repetition of the same image on the side walls. The three images are flat – they are images, after all – but their perpendicular arrangement forms a virtual volume that encircles the viewer. How can one place the viewer inside of the painting rather than before it? A constant preoccupation for Hockney. And he succeeds – we are truly immersed in this forest.

This exceptional hanging only lasted 24 hours, but it was a memorable experience.

*

Bridlington, 2011.

I reserved a small hotel on the beach. It's wintertime. There's not a soul about. David comes to pick me up at the appointed hour and we go straight to the studio, an immense hangar in an industrial estate. All of the iPad drawings from *The Arrival of Spring* are up on the walls, surrounding us – some 50 large sheets of paper covered in vivid, colourful imaginations that are nevertheless so precise, so true. David shows me how he uses the iPad like a portable studio, going out into the surrounding countryside with just this little tablet and returning in the evening with the richest, most vivid paintings there could be. He selects a kind of brush from the menu – a thin or wide line, a blurred cloud without a clear outline, a swarm of tiny dots... I don't know how many kinds of brush tools there are in this application, but they seem limitless. For each mark he plans to make, he chooses a colour from an equally large array, and then he's off, using index finger, thumb, or stylus to draw on the screen. Lines or surfaces appear as he does so, and he saves each step with a click. If he wants to go back to correct something, there is a button for it, and what he erases leaves no trace (which would not be the case on paper or canvas, he points out). 'Brushstrokes' and colours can be superimposed *ad infinitum*, allowing colours to be combined without losing their brilliance (whereas watercolours can barely withstand more than three layers before becoming completely muddled).

Hockney, who loves technical innovations, always finds in them a way of renewing modes of representing reality. He successively adopted the Polaroid, the photocopier, the computer, the touch-sensitive phone, and now the tablet that he uses as a drawing pad. It is always close to hand – he has even had a pocket sewn into the lining of all his suits for it. 'People think that technology has supplanted the hand', he says with a little anticipatory smile. 'But that's not so sure. Look around you – it is a world that's opening up. Look at this drawing: it was made for the screen, with the screen's tools, the screen's light, entirely on the screen. That's not an illusion – that is really what it is.'

David Hockney was quick to see that tablet and telephone screens are particular in that their light comes from behind and passes through the surface that is drawn upon. In any other medium, natural or artificial light hits the surface that it illuminates, but in this one it passes through. Following this train of thought, he takes a moment to draw transparency – a beautiful subject that would be a paradox in any other medium. (A paradox that has often inspired him: pool water mottled with reflections of light, the patio doors of California houses, puddles of water in the countryside...) He draws his ashtray on the iPad: an ashtray made of thick, round, solid glass with four concavities for placing cigarettes. It is amazing to see how, with just a few lines, he conjures the materiality of an object that light passes through, and through which one can see the colour of the table it sits upon and even the grain of the wood, just lightly attenuated and diffracted. The light's reflections in the body of the glass – yellow traces, pinpoints of white.

He is engrossed by the exercise, now taking another thick glass ashtray, this one square, and placing it on a glass table. Behind the ashtray, he places two cylindrical whisky glasses, which he outlines in a very thin white line while a vague bluish trace gives them body and small white cross-hatches on the side indicate reflections of light. He conjures up volume from next to nothing, and it is extraordinarily vivid. Life – that is how you recognise the quality of a still life.

As always, technological innovations bring unexpected effects and paradoxes along with them. As we've seen, the hand is freer than ever on the iPad – it works faster, and thus appears more 'intelligent'. But what was not expected is that the iPad also allows the artist to use a whole range of signs that one might call ready-made – pre-drawn in the same way we speak of prefabricated objects: regular cross-hatching, little round dots of identical size, hashes, and so on. When Hockney selects one of these marks, he gets an effect comparable to how Roy Lichtenstein's use of printing screens produced the ironic distance he held so dear. It is as though, for Lichtenstein, the subject of his paintings were not a given landscape or portrait, but the landscape or portrait drawn by a comic strip artist, printed on paper, and then enlarged to the size of a painting so that the grid of tiny dots that betrays the printing process (which is invisible in comic strip frames) is clearly visible and yet totally artificial. This is how Lichtenstein was able to transform a Mondrian, a Japanese woodblock print, or even a simple water glass into a Lichtenstein. Hockney introduces a similar effect by mixing screens of sorts with a free-hand line – a line as free as that of the Impressionists now suddenly caught up by post-industrial Pointillists.

Among the nibs types the iPad offers Hockney, some are very thin, others very thick, and some create a line of little dots that looks as though it had been drawn by a toothed wheel. Others are blurry and without clear contour, more zones than lines;

Hockney makes abundant use of these to depict the distance, reflections, the effects of mist, and more. Thus, when we look at one of the plates of *The Arrival of Spring* from a distance, we feel as though we're looking at a painter who rivals the Impressionists, or even the great Constable; while from close up, we are in the presence of an ironic, playful, impertinent painting that intelligence has set at a remove from the real – in other words: modern, eminently modern.

Another particular effect of the touchscreen tablet is its ability to enlarge. With a simple movement of one's fingers on the screen, you can change scale – an unremarkable gesture people perform on their phone screen every day, for example, to make text that's too small readable. On the iPad, it allows the artist to work on a drawing in a more detailed, more complex way before printing it on large format paper. Thus, after having worked in detail on a part of a composition he has enlarged, Hockney returns to the initial scale to continue his drawing.

It's clear that Hockney can do whatever he likes with a pencil. But he doesn't do what he doesn't know he wants to do. If some knowledge or technique opens up a new method for him, he greedily dives into it and makes it his own. The result is always Hockney – recognisable at first glance – but it's a new Hockney, fresh, inventive, in tune with the world around him. So long as he's inventing something new, Hockney is enjoying himself, and as long as he's enjoying himself, he keeps us wanting more. His passion for looking (at the landscape, at his friends) becomes our passion to look (at his paintings).

We could make a history of painting based on firsts: the first to paint a smile, the first to paint a tear on a face, the first portrait, the first to abandon tempera for oil paint, the first to use one-point perspective, the first to paint en plein air, the first to paint smoke rising from factory smokestacks, the first to paint rain, and so on. This little game would feature David Hockney a good number of times...

*

We have lunch with all the assistants on a large board set on trestles in the middle of the studio, surrounded by new works that will soon be shown together at the Royal Academy of Arts in London.

Finally, we return to the opulent cottage that is the Bridlington house. David brings me up to the top floor, to the attic that has been converted to a studio – or more precisely today, a projection room. For his latest innovation, Hockney installed three rows of three cameras on a metal frame fixed to the roof of his 4x4. Each camera films as the car slowly advances along a snowy country road. The result is a panorama with more intense presence than anything ever produced on film or in painting. The viewer is surrounded by nature just like in real life: you don't have a single window open before your eyes, but also a sky above your head, a ground beneath your feet, and the feeling that as you move forward, what you see is moving behind you – you don't see it any longer, but it remains in you because it has passed through you. 'Tomorrow, we'll do the film in real life', says David. And indeed, the next day finds us driving slowly along the snow-covered road through Woldgate Woods in the 4 x 4, in the countryside just a few kilometres from Bridlington. We slowly approach the subject of painting – we are surrounded by it. The snow is pristine, its whiteness radiant; a white border highlights and illuminates each branch.

Hockney has transposed onto film what he had already explored in photography with his glued-together Polaroids and in painting with his immense landscapes composed of many small panels. To see better, to see more, to see bigger, to push back the limits of the possible.

III

Los Angeles, 9 December 2014.

David is expecting us at 12:30. We take the usual route, which we now know by heart, as nothing has really changed. At the appointed hour, the door opens and Jean Pierre leads us directly to the studio. Hockney is sitting with an assistant, making a list of books to buy on Amazon. His reading for the day, a biography of Coco Chanel, sits on the table.

David has lost weight. His cheeks have sunken and bear three-day scruff. The collar of his crimson shirt peeks out from a light blue paint-stained sweater. Just one month ago, at his exhibition opening at Pace in New York, he was very elegantly dressed, in a yellow jacket and white cap...

As with almost every visit, Picasso is the first subject of conversation. It's as though this fellowship is always with him. There were two big exhibitions in New York last month: *Picasso and the Camera* at Gagosian and *Picasso & Jacqueline* at Pace. And there were also Matisse's cut-outs at MoMA. He saw everything in three days, during closing hours so as to visit without disturbance. He leafs through the voluminous Gagosian catalogue for us, which is an inexhaustible source of wonder, and then the conversation turns to the 1973 exhibition of Picasso's final works at the Palais des Papes in Avignon. I have a vivid memory of that exhibition and how it was met with unanimous disapproval at the time. Everywhere, you would hear people saying, 'Poor man, he doesn't know what he's doing anymore', and 'He should have stopped already', and 'What a catastrophe!'

Hockney: 'I saw it, too. I was with Douglas Cooper, who kept repeating over and over again, "It's terrible! It's terrible!" I told him, "Douglas, give me time to look, wait for me outside, leave me here with Picasso." And I could finally look, and it was an extraordinary exhibition – an old man speaking to us about old age and death. That was the subject. This old man with his sagging bollocks still had things to say to us. And this last portrait, a few days before his death…'

Douglas Cooper wrote that the paintings in the exhibition were 'incoherent doodles by a frenetic dotard in death's antechamber'. In fact, Cooper was upset that he was no longer being invited to see Picasso, who was too busy painting, and because Jacqueline was overprotective of him. And since he was not a very generous man (Calder called him 'Déguelasse Cooper' to point up his nastiness), he took his revenge in words.

*

Los Angeles, 8 December 2015.

As we enter the studio, an immense screen displays an animated video of an imperial procession depicted on a famous Chinese handscroll housed at the National Art Museum of China. It is gripping. A very light-handed animation makes the columns of soldiers march, the horses bob their heads, the street sweepers sweep – life unfolds. In this vision where there is no single perspective, where the viewer is in several places at once, the world is in movement, free and fantastical. Hockney continues to draw inspiration from the open, intelligent space of Chinese painting.

David is once again immersed in portraiture. 80 new portraits in a year, all in the same format: vertical, approximately 122 x 91 cm, full-body portraits of figures all seated in the same armchair, which is on a platform nearby, in front of a blue curtain and on a green rug. The model sits in a pose that suits them, with legs splayed, clasped, or crossed, and the artist marks the placement of the model's feet on the rug in charcoal so they can easily return to their pose after an interruption. The painter has set his easel below and to the right of the platform. He works standing, his eyes roughly at the centre of the figure before him so the perspective creates minimal distortion. Most are men, a few women, including Celia. (I imagine a retrospective exhibition of all the portraits of Celia made over 40 years. It would be fascinating. I don't know how many he has done – he doesn't either; he says

Maurice Payne is the model he has painted most, and indeed, there he is again in sharp profile, his hair standing on end...) The first painting in this series was a portrait of J.P. seated with elbows on knees and head in hands – exactly the same pose as Van Gogh's old man, housed in the Kröller-Müller Museum in Otterlo. After the accidental death of Hockney's young assistant Dominic Elliott in Bridlington, the artist hastily returned to Los Angeles, leaving behind the subject he had been working on for several seasons: Woldgate Woods. By the time he arrived in Los Angeles, in total distress, he no longer had the heart to paint. When he saw J.P. in this pose, he understood that it also expressed his own feelings, and so he decided to paint him. The very last portrait in the series is a little blond boy, Tacita Dean's son, in a beautiful red tie. The English artist had come to visit Hockney with her young son, and when he saw them, Hockney had the impression of seeing himself at the boy's age. And so he decided to paint him. This undertaking is a vast autobiography in which the painter acts as narrator – an indistinct figure who withdraws from the scene to describe, or rather, to paint it. Some of the models have clearly dressed for the occasion: this one sports multicoloured trousers, giving the painter an opportunity to shine. I see Benedikt Taschen, whom I had met the night before in his observatory overlooking the city; a naturally smiling man, he cultivates a Buster Keaton look here. There is Didier Ottinger, who is preparing David's upcoming exhibition at the Centre Pompidou, Larry Gagosian, who has just dropped by like a friendly neighbour, Gregory before he broke his leg… David Juda is one of the few to have managed to keep a smile. Holding a smile for three days is no mean feat – you have to imagine it comes naturally to him, that geniality is in his nature. And among this gallery of portraits, a banana. David's model wasn't able to make their appointment that day; everything was ready, the painter wanted to paint – he had to paint. So, he placed a banana on the chair in the model's stead and painted it. The exhibition at the Royal Academy of Arts in London would have to be called '81 Portraits and 1 Still-life.'

A model of the museum's rooms sits on the studio table with scaled reproductions of the 81 portraits fixed to the walls in chronological order. They take up the entirety of the available space.

Hockney spent an average of three days on each portrait. He admits that over time he began to do the background and the chair a bit faster, but he used the time saved to work on the figure more. The paintings are made to be seen from a distance, so that one can see several of them together; it really is a gallery of portraits. From close up, the brushstrokes are a little imprecise; the painter has made breathing room – approximations that have life to them and create a stronger image at a distance. We can see that he has focused on relief: how to create a striking impression of relief on a flat image when there is hardly any perspective, only a sort of horizon line formed by the carpet meeting the curtain in the background. It is the same question Giacometti wondered about: how to make the nose emerge from the face? After the Royal Academy, the exhibition will travel to Melbourne.

It is impossible to look at this ensemble without thinking of the morning at the home of the Princess of Guermantes: all of these loved ones he had already painted twenty-odd times in their youth, captured here in the bloating or drying out of age, with an empathetic but uncompromising eye. The painter-narrator of this autobiography is a lucid, even cruel, witness to the passage of time. And when he takes himself as the subject, he is no less unsparing.

*

I notice a drawing by Picasso on the wall: a woman guiding a young child's first steps. Just beside it, another drawing that takes up the exact same subject, treated masterfully by Rembrandt in just a few pen strokes. Hockney never stops looking at the masters. Also pinned to the wall is Van Gogh's old man, in both drawn and painted versions.

Two large horizontal landscapes hang high up at the back of the studio – Hockney's two most recent paintings: a view of the house and pool, and a view of the terrace balcony that runs the length of the house, freshly painted blue (it was previously red and blue). These paintings radiate an incredible presence from the back of the studio – a melody of coloured volumes fitted into one another with an illusion of relief never before achieved to this extent. Hockney has placed an immense mirror on an easel at the back of the studio, doubling the space and creating another view of the paintings hanging on the wall. Above innumerable brushes of all sizes, like flowers in vases, are two signs, warnings of a sort. One says 'Smoking area' (Hockney is a diehard supporter of the right to smoke), and the other addresses us directly: 'All visitors, please please, no photography/video, look with both eyes.' And the two 'O's of 'look' are adorned with eyelashes and large pupils in their centre.

Back at the house, we leaf through a book that Benedikt Taschen just brought him: *Germany 1900*, replete with magnificent colour photographs of cities, streets, and houses that are probably long gone. There's not a single automobile, only streetcars and horses. It's a world that no longer exists. This square in Munich resembles a Canaletto – it's closer to a Chinese scroll than to our contemporary world. Taschen is preparing an enormous book on Hockney, which the two men call the 'Sumo' book.

I work up the courage to ask, in passing, who plays the piano? Nobody, says David, it's a player piano. He opens a little hatch and shows me the device. But it's broken, it doesn't play anymore.

IV

London, July 2016.

At the opening of his exhibition at the Royal Academy of Arts there are actually 82 portraits as well as one still life, though it's not the banana I had seen at the Los Angeles studio. Hockney kept the idea but changed the painting. In lieu of the poor banana, looking a little lonely in its armchair, there is a blue bench that recedes into the background through a distorted perspective like the bench the Virgin Mary sits on in Robert Campin's *Annunciation Triptych*, and upon it sit a red pepper, a lemon, a pear, three tomatoes (or red apples, I don't know), four bananas, and one more lemon – a symphony of shapes and colours.

V

Melbourne, November 2016.

Provisional epilogue. I find the 82 portraits in Melbourne – the only paintings in an immense exhibition focused on the last ten years of the artist's work. Under the title *David Hockney: Current*, the

National Gallery of Victoria has brought together all of his recent technological innovations, such as iPad drawings of spontaneous notes, portraits, everyday objects, landscapes seen from a window, fresh-cut flowers in a vase, and more, forming a kind of diary that unfurls before us. The iPad drawings printed on paper are represented by the two series *The Arrival of Spring* and *Yosemite*; several of the drawings are also exhibited on screens that let the viewer watch the drawing process. As the artist saved each mark he made on the tablet, it is possible to scroll through the stages of the artwork's creation. The 'photographic drawings' are there, too: views of the studio peopled with assistants in multi-point perspective. Here, in inverted perspective, are three of them seated around a table holding playing cards; on the wall behind them hang a painting on the same subject as the present work, but with an observer standing behind them like in the Cézanne painting at the Barnes Collection, the famous *Pearblossom Highway*, a photographic collage from 1986 in which the perspectival distortions are systematically straightened, and the folds of one card player's blue smock hanging from a nail, a final nod to Cézanne. And in a room custom-built for them, the videos of *The Four Seasons* play the selfsame landscape of Woldgate Woods in Yorkshire, filmed four times – in spring, summer, autumn, and winter – by the nine cameras Hockney installed on the roof of his car as it advanced slowly along the forest road, covered in snow here, bathed in light and shadow there. This passion to see the world, always better, always bigger, always differently, is intoxicating.

*

Los Angeles, December 2016.

The Tate Britain and Centre Pompidou retrospective is ready. A reproduction of each painting is affixed to the walls of a physical model of the exhibition rooms. Didier Ottinger asked me to contribute to the catalogue with a text on Hockney and France. I gave a list of entries on this vast subject: biography, the '70s, the Cour de Rohan, the Café de Flore, Shirley Goldfarb, the almost daily visits to the Louvre... I throw out names to elicit reactions: Van Gogh, Ingres, Manet, Degas, Monet, Poussin, Le Lorrain. And from literature as well: Proust, of course, who he read very young, Flaubert, Jarry... And French music: Ravel, Poulenc, Satie... He speaks loquaciously, strolling through his life with levity. J.P. interrupts us for an urgent matter. Following in the footsteps of the greatest painters of the past century, Hockney has just made a label for Château Mouton Rothschild – two glasses toasting the memory of Philippine. The last proof has just arrived and the print order needs to be signed and returned immediately.

*

London, 6 February 2017.

Exhibition opening at Tate Britain. It's all here: the first abstract paintings, the appearance of simplistic figures derived from Dubuffet, the astounding *We Two Boys Together Clinging*, their faces coming into contact like the two Château Mouton glasses, but between their touching mouths, the word 'never' in white paint. The incredible *Cleaning Teeth, Early Evening (10pm) W11* from 1962, where the figures' genitals are tubes of Colgate releasing their white paste. The first paintings from California, the swimming pools... I hear Hockney say, 'It wasn't difficult to paint California – I was the first. But painting Paris after the greats had already done it, that's another thing entirely.' Next is an immense room with the large double portraits painted between 1968 and 1972. It has rightly been pointed out that these double portraits recall Italian annunciations. You can see it: Henry Geldzahler enthroned on a massive grey sofa, facing straight out toward the viewer, and the angel Christopher strapped into his raincoat entering in profile; Celia and Ossie in *Mr and Mrs Clark and Percy* (Percy is the white cat on Ossie's lap, an echo of the lilies in the vase on the table. A frightened cat can be seen running away in Lotto's annunciation, but here the cat calmly bathes in the sunlight streaming in through the window like rays of Holy Spirit). Next is a room lined with drawings from throughout Hockney's career, and then the Polaroid collages, where space breaks down only to put itself back together again. (I remember the Kasmin exhibition in London in the early '80s – I went with Vera Russell, who introduced me to Hockney. Standing before the fragmentation of faces and bodies, I brought up Proust, and Hockney immediately followed suit, explaining how these compositions of snapshots brought time into the work.) The photo collage room ends with the famous 1986 *Pearblossom Highway*, which naturally opens onto an ensemble entitled *Experiences of Space*, bringing together the house interiors and Los Angeles landscapes, then the large canyons and the first Yorkshire landscapes with their horizon lines at the very top of the paintings, like in Gauguin's Brittany paintings, and finally the Yorkshire forests in all seasons, though the very large painting shown at the Royal Academy isn't among them. Then there are the videos of the four seasons, and finally, the whole of *The Arrival of Spring* in charcoal on paper, with its prodigious mastery of lighting in the undergrowth in black and white, and the latest paintings of the Montcalm Avenue house's garden and balcony, which were in the studio when I last visited.

Chris Stephen, who curated the exhibition at Tate Britain, says to Hockney: 'This is the first time a living artist has had a retrospective at the Tate.' One more first for David Hockney. 'Sure, but the exhibition in Paris this June will be even bigger', replies Hockney, for whom nothing is ever big enough.